Hi!

My name's Carl (usually known as Beechy). I'm an Essex boy born and bred. At 18 I changed my mind about joining the armed forces when I met Jesus and realised that God was calling me to fight a different sort of battle. Over the next few years I became convinced that God was calling me and my wife Karen to plant a new church. We didn't have a clue what we were doing! But we set to work and experienced at first hand the power of God to change lives radically.

After becoming senior pastor of a large church, I felt God wanted me to work towards seeing men across the UK turn to Jesus. It's a big dream! It meant a move to Bath in 2006 to become the National Director for Christian Vision for Men (CVM). And a lot of time on the road since then, meeting men across the UK.

Karen and I have two girls, Emily and Annie. I love spending time with the family, fishing, cycling, walking our German Shepherd dog (nickname ASBO) in the mud, lifting weights and eating curry. And that's about it. What you see is what you get.

In this magazine you'll find some real life stories of men. Three of these men are still around and I'm proud to call them my friends. The other men are characters I've read about in the Bible. I'm convinced they've all of them got loads to teach us – from their failures as well as their successes. Enjoy!

Carl

CLIVE

'I WAS THE FAT KID

Clive was the classic fat kid who was bullied at school. Aged 11, he tipped the scales at a massive 14 stone. No one wanted him on their team because he always came last. He struggled with asthma and missed lots of lessons, so was never more than average at schoolwork. Moving schools didn't help. He dreamed of being popular, but felt he was always going to be picked on. 'I simply had nothing to offer to make friends with anyone. Nothing to offer to be accepted.'

Then Clive discovered martial arts. He was good at it. He slimmed down, got fit, trained six days a week. He became a good-looking teen and popular – and turned into a bully himself.

'Through martial arts I realised I could defend myself, but then I started to look for fights to prove I could take care of myself.'

Clive became obsessed, eventually training in over 30 different kinds of martial arts. He left school at 15 and started a plumbing apprenticeship, but his ambition was to become a martial arts instructor.

'Karate, kung fu, Bruce Lee's jeet kune do... I trained in as many as I could. I became the instructor's top student and moved in with him. My parents divorced around this time and my instructor became my role model. But although martial arts is about discipline, I got deeply involved in drinking and fighting.'

EVERYONE LAUGHED AT...'

At 21 Clive took a job as a nightclub bouncer. 'I got into horrendous fights – but I enjoyed the violence and the praise I got for hurting people.'

Life started to get even more hair-raising when Clive's girlfriend got pregnant. And, on the inside, Clive was experiencing a hollow emptiness. He began searching for something more meaningful in his life – a search which led him to consulting tarot cards, psychics and mediums.

He left the doorman job, achieved his goal of becoming an instructor, married and tried to settle down with Debbie. By the time he was in his late 20s they had two sons – Zack and Brandon. As he turned 30, his career began to really take off – leading to appearances on TV and international travel to competitions and demonstrations.

'I saw that what it took to stand out from the rest of the martial arts instructors was to be entertaining, a bit of a personality. So I played up to the cameras, acted the fool, and I found they kept coming back for more.'

Clive's marriage had been rocky for some time and when he was 33 he and Debbie separated. He started a relationship with Karen, a young martial arts instructor. During this time Clive had a number of encounters that seemed bizarre… including meetings with no fewer than three church ministers who also practised martial arts. One of these claimed to have had a vision about Clive and another challenged him about knowing Jesus Christ.

'I'd always sort of believed in God, even though I was going to mediums. But I knew nothing about Jesus.'

A conversation with one minister ended with Clive saying 'the sinner's prayer' to follow Jesus. Despite being counselled otherwise, Clive walked into the house waving a Bible, completely freaking out Karen. Life became very difficult!

Three months later Clive suggested they might both go on an Alpha course. Karen agreed. But when it came to signing up, they discovered that it was held locally on the same night that Clive

'I LEARNED TO ACHIEVE TO WIN, TO PUSH MYSELF – AND I'VE ACCOMPLISHED SO MUCH BUT KNOWING CHRIST IS THE MOST IMPORTANT THING IN MY LIFE.'

had his two boys to stay over. Karen said she would go anyway – to disprove it!

'But by week three she came home saying she knew it was all true, and she had given her life to Christ!'

Some years on, Clive and Karen – now married – are both still very active on the martial arts scene and involved in church life. Maintaining their links with the martial arts world has earned them a fair amount of criticism from other churchgoers.

'There's no doubt that a lot of martial arts are connected with the occult,' says Clive. 'People don't realise, for example, that a lot of the salutations and mantras involve worship of the sun and moon. That's why I choose to work now with the more westernised forms and leave others alone.

'Martial arts is the second biggest participatory sport in Britain – the first being fishing. It's going to be a real turn-off to people if we say that they can't practise martial arts and be a Christian. We just need to educate people about how to do it.

'Obviously I have thought long and hard about whether I should continue in martial arts. I know that I could just walk away from it. I can live without it. For years I was obsessed with martial arts, with my diet, the way I looked. But not any more. And any time I can witness for Christ, I will.

'I know I've had issues with pride that I've had to deal with. Recently I pulled out of taking part in three martial arts films because I felt that I would be bringing glory to myself, not to God. I know that I love being in front of the cameras, and God has brought me to my knees about it. I always thought I could handle any fights – but the spiritual battles I am in because of following Christ are far harder than anything I've ever been in.'

Clive is keenly aware of being a role model to those he teaches. Currently he, Karen and fellow teacher Brendan have about 110 martial arts students in the Swindon, Newbury and Thatcham areas. About 50 are kids in the 5-12 age group.

'We run an educational programme for the kids. It's not just about the physical moves, but it's about good behaviour. Because I teach them to kick, punch and throw, they respect me. So I work with checklists. These cover everything from cleaning their teeth and tidying their rooms to treating their parents well. In my classes, if the kids  don't have ticks in the boxes for good behaviour at home, they can't do the grading.'

Clive says he is grateful for what martial arts has given him.

'I was the fat kid everyone laughed at. I have no paper qualifications. But through martial arts I learned to achieve, to win, to push myself – and I've accomplished so much. But knowing Christ is the most important thing in my life.' GB

Who? **Visionary and faithful man of God who survived the flood**
When? **Pre-history**
Why? **For insights about radical faith and obedience**
Where? **Genesis 6—9**

Noah

HE SAW THE JOB THROUGH TO THE END.

Let's set the scene.

One day an angel of God or an audible voice from heaven – take your pick – tells you to build a spaceship capable of carrying your family and all the animals in Bristol Zoo into space. You are to build it in your back garden and get all your supplies from the local hardware shop. At which point in the day would you go and see your GP?

To put Noah's task in perspective, it was to build an enormous boat using local materials, with the aim of storing two of each kind of animal for a year – a task that was every bit as outlandish for Noah a few thousand years ago as it would be for you to build a spaceship now.

It's an absolutely staggering story of faith and belief. And a story that's been misused. I believe it's been massively diluted by its use as a children's story.

When I first went to church at 18, I had a row in a Christian bookshop because I couldn't believe that the only books you could get on Noah's ark were kids' stories!

VIOLENCE WAS ENDEMIC; THE ATMOSPHERE DARK AND OPPRESSIVE; HEDONISM RULED. SOUND FAMILIAR?

I remember telling the staff that they were out of order. How could you sell a book about mass destruction and death to kids? As a newbie in the Church I couldn't get my head round it. Still can't, actually. Noah's story is one of gut-churning horror, triumph over adversity, heroic faith, dogged grit and determination. Tough stuff. It's not for the faint-hearted, and definitely not the children's bedtime story we have made it.

Noah was a man of faith who stood rock solid in God in a time when no one else could be bothered or had the guts to. He honoured God when everyone else chose to ignore him. He stood his ground, probably under extreme ridicule.

He glimpsed the bigger picture and saw the job through to the end, despite the cost to his reputation and livelihood. Let's get rid of the fluff. Noah lived in a time when God moved in devastating holy power and judgement in a way we won't see again until Jesus comes back. The story also contains what is possibly the saddest verse in the whole Bible: 'The LORD was grieved that he had made man on the earth, and his heart was filled with pain' (Genesis 6:6).

Noah lived in a knife-edge time. Everything around him was spinning out of control. Violence was endemic; the atmosphere dark and oppressive; hedonism ruled. Sound familiar? But Noah remained blameless.

You and I know how hard it is to keep pure. You know how hard it is not to look where you shouldn't look and not to go where you shouldn't go. You know how hard it is not to stumble into lust, or allow anger to rise up, or let bitterness and revenge take hold of you. Noah fought those same battles and won. Probably through gritted teeth.

Was there a secret to his ability to remain distinctive? Look at Genesis 6:22: 'Noah did everything just as God commanded him.'

That's the key to being *righteous*!

Have you got that quality? I'm talking about a steely determination to go where God sends you and do as he tells you – no matter what! Are you out of that mould?

Now think about a few of the facts. When Noah is first mentioned he was 500 years old. When Noah entered the ark he was 600! We don't know at what point (between Genesis 5:32 and 6:21) he got his orders. But it may have taken up to 100 years to build the ark!

Details aside, this was a long journey of unrelenting faith, single-minded focus and perseverance.

Bear with me for a couple more facts.

Noah got on board the ark on the seventeenth day of the second month (Genesis 7:11–13). He got out on the twenty-seventh day of the second month of the following year (Genesis 8:14,16). Now that's some test of a man's mettle! That's 370 days of waking up every day in a foul, stinking, messy wooden box, wondering if you will ever get out… wondering if you will ever see life on solid ground again.

I expect there were domestic tensions. I expect they all got up each other's nostrils at times as much as the stench did. Certainly Noah had his flaws. He probably spent the 370 days with dirty hands and a sore back. But he stuck at it!

Follow that. GB

QUESTIONS

Do you have anything like the grit of Noah?

Do you do all God commands – despite threats of ridicule or embarrassment?

Do you see a vision through over the long term?

Are you resistant to the pressures around you?

When you face ridicule for your faith, how do you respond?

Are you a man who grieves God? Or a man who gives God joy?

ACTIONS

Learn from a man who got it right when the chips were down.

Make a decision to be God's man and not a crowd follower.

Make a decision to see a job through, no matter what.

Learn to focus not on what people think about you… but on what God thinks about you.

Joseph

HE KEPT HIMSELF PURE. . . .

There's no doubt that Joseph had something special going for him – and I'm not just talking about the Old Testament equivalent of a Versace coat! Thanks to a few songs and plays, the coat of many colours is pretty much what most people know him for, and that's a real shame. So we're going to get past the coat and get learning from a man who could be annoying and appear arrogant, but who displayed incredible self-discipline and never gave in to circumstances.

Joseph was the eleventh of Jacob's twelve sons, born to Rachel who just happened to be Jacob's favourite wife. So it follows that Joseph was Jacob's favourite son. Bad parenting by Jacob led to Joseph having more than a rough time at the hands of his brothers. My advice is to resist having a favourite son or daughter; it only causes long term hurt and rejection and does the siblings in.

Anyway, the coat – a gift to Joseph from his doting dad – makes an appearance in Genesis 37. As a result of that and consistently uneven treatment, his brothers get so fed up that they sell Joseph into slavery. OK, so Joseph relaying a dream to his brothers which suggested that he was superior and that they would all bow to him didn't help matters! But, in a sense, the rot had already set in by that time.

TEMPTATION WILL COME OVER THE HORIZON AND IT MIGHT WELL BE IN THE FORM OF A DROP-DEAD ATTRACTIVE WOMAN IN A MINISKIRT

The adventure begins. In brief, Joseph goes from being a highly trusted slave in the house of a senior government official (Potiphar) in Egypt, to being unfairly placed in prison, to being second-in-command of the whole of Egypt. Some journey, eh?

Finally, his brothers (who thought he was dead) come across him in Egypt where they go to find food during a famine. Joseph had come up with the bright idea of storing food in Egypt after interpreting Pharaoh's dream warning about impending famine. The brothers bow to him, just as predicted by Joseph years previously.

Here are four lessons to deal with:
1 We know Joseph is young, good-looking and well built. Women fancy him – in particular, his boss' wife. Not good. But does Joseph – in his sexual prime and yet still immature – succumb and take her to bed? No! He holds his ground and resists.

He doesn't hold the line primarily because he respects his boss, although that's what he refers to first in Genesis 39:8. He holds the line because to bed the boss' wife would be an offence against God! And there was no way Joseph is going to hurt God when he knows that everything he hopes for in life depends on him.

Ultimately, whenever we fall, it's God we hurt; which is why in his psalm of confession after committing adultery and murder (Psalm 51) David tells God it is only against him that he has sinned…

Joseph has to resist more than once! Potiphar's wife doesn't let up on the poor bloke. In fact, she nags him for sex! In the end, there's only one thing for it. Joseph does a runner (Genesis 39:12).

Now, that's character! How easy would it have been to give in? After all, no one would ever know – would they? Of course, what you really are is what you are when no one else is looking.

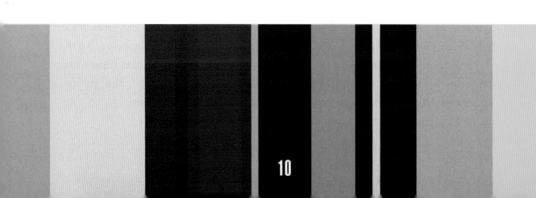

Joseph knew that God would see it all and that's what kept him pure.

Guys, you can be sure that if ever there's a time when everything is going well in life and God's favour is resting on you, that's when temptation will come over the horizon and it might well be in the form of a drop-dead attractive woman in a miniskirt. If that happens, run boys! Run to the hills and don't look back! That fleeting moment of physical pleasure could cost you everything.

Just have in mind two things. Firstly, it may be a test from God to see if you are ready for the next stage. Or, secondly, it could be sent from Satan to destroy you. In either case, run! I've seen many a good man destroyed because he took a second look. Don't join their ranks!

2 Did you know that when God's favour is on you it blesses everyone near you as well? Just as sin from one person can pollute an entire organisation or family, so faithfulness from one person can bring peace and blessing. Read it for yourself! Genesis 39 is clear on the matter. The faithfulness of Joseph brings a blessing on the whole of Potiphar's household. What implications does that have for a man of God who holds the line in a business or in his family in issues of moral and spiritual integrity? I'll leave you to draw your own conclusions.

3 The situation gets even worse for Joseph. Falsely accused of raping his boss' wife, he's thrown into the dungeon. Joseph still holds the line. He could have got the hump with God when he was thrown into prison. He could have decided to believe the lie that God had abandoned him. He could have turned away from developing into a good man. Instead, he chooses to walk the noble path. He faces his false imprisonment with dignity.

4 Joseph was, of course, vindicated in the end. He was even reconciled to the brothers that sold him out. Don't make the mistake, though, of thinking that just because it all happened within a few pages in the Bible that it happened quickly in real time.

Joseph was at least 37 when he met up with his brothers again. (He was 30

IF THAT HAPPENS, RUN BOYS! RUN TO THE HILLS AND DON'T LOOK BACK!

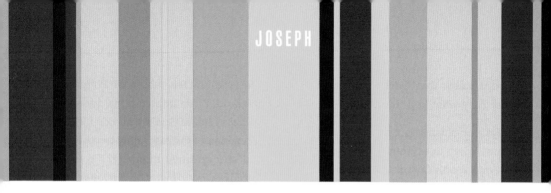

when he entered Pharaoh's service in Genesis 41:46 and then there was at least another seven years before the brothers turned up.) Given that he was first sold at about 17 years of age, that's 20 years of dealing with rejection and hurt. A long time to dream of revenge and retribution. It would have been so easy for Joseph to put his brothers through a living hell and lose any chance of reconciliation.

Most of us men are good at plotting revenge. We are good at fantasising about the downfalls of our enemies. We relish the thought of seeing someone get what they deserve. We love TV programmes and movies that show justice being meted out to people. Plenty of best-selling novels involve violent revenge. However, listen up: **revenge and following Jesus are completely incompatible**. You've just got to leave feuds where they belong... consigned to history, wiped from the 'to do' list. As soon as Joseph saw that his brothers were genuine, that's what Joseph did – and it led to a beautiful future. GB

QUESTIONS

How would you feel if you were wrongly accused? How would you handle it?
How do you fight temptation? When is running the only solution?
How do you deal with the desire to gain revenge?

ACTIONS

Make it a habit to be first to apologise.
Deal with long term feuds before they spin out of control.
Make a decision to stay faithful to God even when he feels absent.
Run from sexual temptation... and don't look back!

DAVID

HE HAD FIRE IN HIS BELLY...

David was an alpha male.

He came to prominence by taking down Goliath on the battlefields. Cutting off his head and holding it high in front of the enemy hordes of panicking Philistines, he showed that his courage and his heart for God were bigger than his teenage frame and penchant for poetry suggested...

He was a leader of leaders. While serving as an officer in King Saul's army he gained a fearsome reputation as a brutal killer of thousands and a gifted military strategist. He became a revered hero of the people.

When the people started the chant of 'Saul has killed his thousands but David his tens of thousands', it didn't exactly help the tense relationship between Saul and David. Saul got so eaten up by jealousy that he tried to kill David more than once. Some insecurity!

Eventually David was forced to hide in the desert. Against all the odds and assisted by a ragtag gang of guys reminiscent of the *A Team*, he eventually wiped out the marauding Amalekites and became King of Judah (the southern kingdom). Then, after taking out Ishbosheth – son of Saul and ruler of Israel – David became king of a newly united kingdom, ruling from 1005 BC to 965 BC.

David was a killer, poet, harpist, swordsman, statesman, inspirational general and serial lover.

Life and passion flowed through his veins and adrenalin was his life force. Picture David and you don't conjure up the image of a man contemplating his navel. You imagine a man with fire in his belly, sword in one hand and chariot reins in the other, leading the charge.

He fought alongside three warrior brothers, all of whom had superhuman abilities to wage war. There was Jashobeam, who once killed 800 enemy warriors in one battle. Then there was Eleazar, the warrior who stood alone beside David killing Philistines with his sword in such numbers that he only stopped when he could no longer lift his sword. Finally there was Shammah, who wasn't against taking on a whole field of enemies all by himself. I haven't got room to tell you about the band of brothers that were 'the 30' and about Abishai and the 300 he killed with one spear...

The point is this. David was their leader and their brother. At one point, talking about the men closest to him, David refused to drink water even though he was dehydrated to illustrate that the water was to him as precious as the blood of his fellow warriors. He was a giant among men and as fiercely godly as he was fiercely violent.

And then he got derailed. Not by a beautiful woman in a miniskirt. Not even by going where he shouldn't have gone. He was derailed by his heart. Let me explain...

David probably already knew Bathsheba. Her husband Uriah was one of David's elite men, part of the band of brothers who was able to walk freely past the personal bodyguard and speak face to face with David.

DAVID WAS TRYING TO FIND A SAFE TIME TO SIN. WITH GOD THERE IS NO SUCH THING.

Uriah was not in the inner circle of 'the three' but he was close. He was used to David asking him for military opinions and was probably as comfortable in the king's presence for a chat as fighting by his side on the battlefield. He was loyal unto death. Shame the king wasn't.

We can assume that David knew Uriah's wife, Bathsheba. In fact, it's obvious that she lived near the palace. Near enough to be seen quite clearly by David when he took his stroll.

Maybe David had taken a stroll at various times in the past. Perhaps he got to know when she would be taking her purification baths. Perhaps he had taken a wrong turning in his mind months before. Yes, this is all speculation – but it seems quite possible to me.

David had no hesitation in sending his guards to fetch her with the sole purpose of having sex with her. And he had no hesitation on finding out that she was pregnant in hatching a cover-up plan that was ruthless and cold and meant the death of his loyal brother warrior. He even sent a gift to Uriah before plotting his death. Refusing to drink water to demonstrate love for his brother warriors sounds a bit lame now, doesn't it?

I want to go a stage further.

Bathsheba had just had her period. That's why she was bathing – in accordance with the customs as described in Leviticus 15:19–24 and 2 Samuel 11:4. In other words, David actually slept with her when it was pretty much safe to go for it without much danger of pregnancy. There was probably only a one per cent chance of her getting pregnant.

David was trying to find a safe time to sin. **With God there is no such thing.** Sin sexually and repetitively without dealing with it and it will come out. David had a dark centre in his heart and it was about to seriously undo him. Sin leads to sin.

Bathsheba did get pregnant and their son died as a direct result of his adultery. His kingdom was never the same again. His family was ripped apart by heartache, rape and murder. He saw his sons get killed and the nation who

HE HAD TO LEARN THE HARD WAY TO DEAL WITH HIS DARK CENTRE.

once loved him turn against him in rebellion. Even his own son Absalom turned on him, going head to head in battle. Absalom, who should have been David's successor, inherited all the worst traits of his father as well as some of the good ones. But, instead of repenting like David, he just went from bad to worse and ended up being stabbed to death by his father's soldiers.

Sin has harsh consequences.

I don't want to finish there because thankfully David didn't end badly. He had to learn the hard way to deal with his dark centre. But David finished well. He repented, got past the turmoil and led the people as well as he could. He is remembered in the Hebrews 11 'hall of fame' and was even quoted by Jesus.

QUESTIONS

What are the pitfalls of being an alpha male?
And the plus points?

ACTIONS

Be thankful for the cross!
If you are in trouble right now, deal with it immediately.
If you are being derailed, don't do an Absalom. Do a David.
Put it right and live! Or you will be undone.

Jon

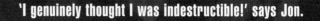

'I WAS A MONSTER

'I genuinely thought I was indestructible!' says Jon.

And you can see why he might have thought that. By his early 30s he'd pretty much done it all:

- regularly drinking himself into oblivion with up to 12 pints of strong lager and two bottles of wine every night;

- engaging in a string of broken relationships including affairs with several married women;

- cooking up dodgy business ventures that saw him alternately sleeping rough and penniless or loaded and driving a Mercedes sports car;

- facing an armed gang of heavies who were calling in loans;

- plotting his own suicide — a plan thwarted at the eleventh hour by a mysterious stranger;

- crashing at 90 mph so spectacularly that it should have wiped him off the planet, but he pulled through major surgery and over a month in a coma *and* losing the sight of one eye, to joke and play the field again.

AND MONEY WAS MY GOD...'

'I was a monster,' Jon Pedley remembers. 'I had no morals. I was greedy and selfish. Money was my god. I earned it, worshipped it and wasted it. But I was so unhappy. There was an aching hole in my life.'

Jon takes no pride in his past but regularly recalls the details in gratitude to a God who rescued him and gave him a brand new life. He unashamedly describes his deep concern for those who don't yet know God as being the motivating factor now in getting him out of bed in the mornings.

'Actually, I'd always believed in some kind of higher being and there was churchgoing in my upbringing. But I'd thrown it all away when I left home at 16, apart from using God as an occasional fruit machine – chucking a prayer into the slot as I passed, not really believing it was heard, but just in case.

'But it was finally in Jesus Christ that I found a real hero – a hero I admire as much as love. What a revolutionary! He's everything I aspire to, yet perhaps the Church's best-kept secret and so much in our society conspires to hide him from us.'

Despite the dramatic highs and lows of Jon's life, it wasn't one of the very real crisis points that brought him to faith in Christ.

There was, for example, the suicide that never happened. At 22 when his business went bust and he was sleeping rough in railway stations and office doorways in London, he decided he just didn't want to wake up any more. With some stolen money he bought a stash of sleeping pills and a litre of whisky and wrote suicide notes to his lover and his parents. On a last drinking binge he was chatting up two girls in a pub, aiming at some casual sex before he died. But in the pub loo he was stopped in his tracks by the insistent message from an embarrassed elderly man he'd never met before and he's never seen since.

'I was told to come and tell you... I know you're in trouble, but you're not to give up... because... Jesus loves you... he told me to come and tell you that.'

The dumbfounded Jon went back to his hotel, threw the pills away and woke the next morning – with a headsplitting hangover, but still alive.

'JESUS WAS DEEPLY REBELLIOUS, FUNDAMENTALLY REVOLUTIONARY, UNCOMPROMISING AND INDISPUTABLY STRONG.'

That incident might perhaps have driven someone else to faith, but not Jon. He kept up his drunken lifestyle, managed to resume a career in selling software packages for call centres, got married, had two children, embarked on an affair with his wife's best friend and got divorced.

Even a horrendous life-threatening crash didn't make Jon search for God.

'No, I came back worse, determined to be the best salesman, the hardest drinker, the life and soul of the party.'

But, a couple of years and a few more broken relationships further on, Jon started looking for something to fill the emptiness in his life. And it was a visit to St Mike's Church in Aberystwyth that stopped him in his tracks.

'I looked into the faces of the people there and could see God in their lives. They had something I didn't – and I wanted it. I tried desperately to hate them, to find a reason to trash what they stood for – but I couldn't.'

It was an Alpha course at St Mike's that finally brought Jon face to face with Jesus.

'I'd always classified him as a bit of a wimp, dressed in white and with a facial hair issue. But in the Bible I found he was someone I could not only relate to but admire. He was deeply rebellious, fundamentally revolutionary, uncompromising and indisputably strong.

'In February 2004, aged 35, I finally stopped fighting him and asked Jesus to come into my life, to take away the hurt and make me whole. And he did! No bang, no thunder and no lightning!'

With a grin that lights up his face, Jon describes walking through town with his six-year-old son a week later:
–'Happy new you, Dad.'
–'What, son?'
–'Happy new you, Dad. You're like a brand new person!'

Exactly that! Jon has discovered the value of stronger and truer relationships. He's happily teetotal and celibate. And is growing in his new faith at a rate of knots, due to the two hours daily he devotes to prayer and reading any good Christian books he can get his hands on, and to the strong supportive family at St Mike's.

'I was so scared that becoming a Christian would mean being an un-person... now I look back and can't believe how black and white my old life was next to the fantastic technicolor experience of knowing God and living how he made me to live.'

Experiencing forgiveness from others and from God for his wayward past continues to challenge Jon. He has some huge regrets – in particular an abortion he arranged for a girlfriend – and then there's the undoubted harm he has caused his two children. But he's trusting the God who can make all things new. And his overwhelming sense of gratitude to the Jesus he now follows makes him a natural, vibrant and infectious communicator of the gospel to everyone he meets. And he's sure got a story to tell! GB

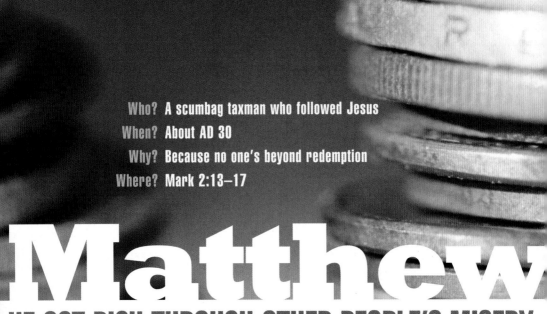

Who? A scumbag taxman who followed Jesus
When? About AD 30
Why? Because no one's beyond redemption
Where? Mark 2:13–17

Matthew

HE GOT RICH THROUGH OTHER PEOPLE'S MISERY...

You know when you are onto something good. You feel it in the pit of your stomach. Sometimes your heart rate goes up. It's a gut feeling that's hard to explain or put into words.

I had that feeling when someone took me aside and asked me if I wanted to go to India with him to 'do some ministry'. I leapt at it. As soon as he asked me I just knew I had to get on that plane with him! Yes, OK, so I probably should have prayed and I probably should have chatted it over with a few people... but sometimes you just know, don't you?

When you get that feeling, what you do with it is up to you. You can walk away or you can jump in with two feet.

That's what you get when you look at the encounter of Levi with Jesus.

You probably know Levi better as Matthew, the author of the first Gospel.

He was a tax collector. That meant he got rich through other people's misery. He was a corrupt figure of hate.

Jesus had been around in Capernaum for a bit doing stuff and so Levi knew who Jesus was. His reputation had gone before him as a doer of miracles and a teacher well worth listening to – as opposed to some of the raging lunatic gurus of doom that were often marauding around at the time.

So Levi had probably been sussing Jesus out. He had probably come to the conclusion that he was the real deal after all. Being the man he was, Levi could no doubt spot a fraud at 30 paces and knew a Walter Mitty when he saw one; after all, he probably was something of one himself!

So now Jesus comes past and doesn't so much ask the million dollar question as put a blunt proposition before him:

'Follow me.'

Put that in context. 'Follow me' means:
–Leave your life of wealth accumulation.
–Leave behind your friends and family.
–Leave behind everything you know and trust and start your life over again.
–Oh, and by the way... it will cost you everything.

I guess that was a pit of the stomach moment. Levi went for it.

What about you? You see, I think we all face moments like that. They don't just come when we first decide to follow Jesus. There are times along the way when he calls us to further adventure and to choose whether to lay everything down to follow him.

Levi changed his name to Matthew and started over. He then went on to pour out his heart for the gospel.

Early Church tradition has it that he went as far afield as Ethiopia in his quest to spread the news about Jesus, and got martyred by being run through by a halberd (a two-pronged spear) in the city of Nadaba in AD 60. That's a far cry from being a taxman in Capernaum.

I'm fully aware that some of you out there have had that pit of the stomach moment but let it pass you by. Some of you think that you have lost your moment.

Let me tell you something. The God I serve always finishes what he starts. Always! You may have missed that moment in time but if you sincerely tell him that you will follow him when he calls then he will call you again. God loves to use faithful and willing men. So be one!

Or perhaps you don't want to make the commitment to follow Jesus wholeheartedly and do whatever he asks you. That is your privilege and your choice. All I do know is that on the day you meet Jesus in all his risen glory, you may just feel more than a pang of regret!

There's one more thing I need to say about this. In the eyes of the people, Levi was a complete scumbag. He was the lowest of the low, an extortionist, devoid of compassion for people. And God chose him.

You might feel like you are carrying more baggage than a 747 and have more history than the British Museum. You might feel that you are beyond any usefulness to God. Be assured that those sorts of feelings are enemy lies. Believe none of it. If he can use Levi and turn his life around then don't be so proud as to think he can't do the same for you!

QUESTIONS

What does it mean for you to respond to Jesus' 'Follow me'?
What's holding you back from jumping in with both feet to serve Jesus?

ACTION

Do whatever's necessary to de-clutter your spirit so that you're in a state of readiness to go on an adventure with God.

Who? A short bloke who had Jesus as a dinner guest

When? In the days when Jesus was walking around the earth doing good

Why? A must-read story for anyone who needs God's grace!

Where? Luke 19:1–10

Zacchaeus

HE GAVE BACK ALL HE HAD STOLEN — AND THEN SOME..

I can tell this story in about three lines.

There's this short bloke in Jericho. He's a corrupt taxman out to mess people up for the benefit of his own lifestyle. He climbs a tree to get a glimpse of Jesus. Jesus tells him to get out of the tree. Jesus goes to his house and has a big slap-up meal with him and all his dodgy mates. Wham! Zacchaeus is sorted out for all time. He gives all the stolen money back – and more. The end.

Well… ten lines!

Now that's what I call a close encounter with God. You might want to picture the scene in *Independence Day* with Will Smith at this point.

There's two things I want us to get hold of from this story:
• Jesus called Zacchaeus by name.
• He went to his home.

There's power in calling someone by his or her name. Where I grew up everyone had the same name: 'Mate'. In fact, the only time someone used your actual name was if you were in trouble! Whenever I heard 'Carl!' being called out, I knew I was in for it!

Not so with Jesus. He calls us by name for an entirely different reason. He calls us by name because he is for us not against us and knows everything about us. In fact, the Bible says that he has been watching over us since before we were born and knows every day planned for us until the day we die (Psalm 139).

That's got to give you some kind of reassurance, hasn't it? You might be reading this on the train as you go to work, or over a mug of tea before walking out of the door. Wherever you are and whoever you are, Jesus is calling you by name and knows all about your day before you even start it! He knows all the good stuff, all the bad stuff and all the stuff you haven't even done yet... and still calls you by name!
I wonder how Zacchaeus felt when he heard his name being called. It was probably a mixture of feeling pretty unnerved and pretty special.

This encounter tells us something very important... and it's a message that still stands today. When Jesus came, he came for everyone, whether you are a thief, a duke, a dentist or a street cleaner. Zacchaeus knew this the moment he heard his name being called... and he got right out of the tree!

Most people thought Zacchaeus was beyond all help and frankly there wasn't much love for him in Jericho! But no one is past it, in Jesus' view, and no one is unlovable... and that's why he called out to Zacchaeus. Pretty amazing, eh? Don't you just love that about Jesus... he's always going for those no one else wants to know about; always sitting down for dinner with the people others want to avoid. Imagine having Jesus come to your house for dinner. Just incredible! The Son of God, who was there at the beginning of time, actually went to Zacchaeus' house for a bite to eat!

This is even more amazing: Jesus wants to come to your house right now. He wants to be involved in every area of your life and help you get things straight. He wants to help you to be the man you know you ought to be! For Zacchaeus, the meal ended up with him giving back everything he had stolen and then some! GB

QUESTIONS

What would it mean for you to have Jesus come to your house? Right now?

ACTIONS

Well, Jesus is waiting to come on in... dare you open the door?

Who? **Astute politician and born survivor**
When? **Something like AD 33, close to the time of Jesus' death**
Why? **Because men need backbone**
Where? **Luke 22:66 – 23:25**

PILATE

HE CHOSE THE QUIET LIFE...

All too often men try to pass the buck. For a quiet life. Or to protect their corner. For revenge. Or just because…

Have you ever watched one of those reality shows where only the fittest survive such as *The Apprentice*? Have you noticed how, when people are in a tight corner, everyone tries to ditch the blame? It's startling how people who were patting each other on the back one minute are stabbing each other in the same place less than five minutes later!

Pretty distasteful behaviour. You see it everywhere, from the football pitch to the boardroom. People just looking out for number one.

Let me tell you: **that sort of behaviour is completely incompatible with following Jesus**. When we finally meet the Lord that kind of track record could be our undoing.

So what about Pilate? You could say that Pilate was in a 'lose/lose' situation. It's one thing to preside over a court of law, but to pass judgement in the kind of situation in which Pilate found himself was something else.

Take a look at the proceedings as described in Luke 23.

First Pilate asks the question: 'Are you the king of the Jews?'

YOU ARE PART OF SOMETHING MUCH BIGGER. BIGGER THAN YOU CAN EVER IMAGINE.

I think at this moment Pilate is just doing his bit and playing to the crowd. So when Jesus says, 'Yes, I am… ' Pilate thinks, 'Well, OK then, that's fine, I asked the question, I got an answer!' All he wants to do is let him go and get out of there. The quiet life beckons!

But once again the people kick off and let it slip that Jesus came from Galilee. Pilate has his way out! If Jesus started his troublemaking in Galilee then it's Herod's problem and not his. Round one to Pilate, who probably retired for a glass of red!

But Herod doesn't get anywhere with Jesus and packs him off back to Pilate, who gets everyone together and tells them there is no charge against Jesus. But, as you can read for yourself, the crowd bays for blood! Even with the promise that Pilate would have Jesus punished (read here: grotesque, incredibly violent beating) the crowd still want Jesus to be nailed to a cross.

And so what does Pilate do? There is no basis for a charge. No basis for the death penalty. Not really even a basis for a beating! Well… Pilate has him killed. Why? Because he wasn't his own man. He was more concerned for his popularity and longevity than for justice.

In John's account (John 19) we get to listen in to a really amazing conversation between Pilate and Jesus. It takes place behind closed doors, just as Pilate is starting to get scared.

–Pilate: 'Where do you come from?'
–Jesus: No answer.
–Pilate: 'Don't you realise that I have the power to have you set free or killed?'
–Jesus (looking Pilate in the eye): 'You would have no power over me if it hadn't been given to you from above!'

That's a killer response from Jesus. What he was saying is this: 'You may think you have the upper hand. You may think you are in control. But the truth is you are part of something much bigger. Bigger than you can ever imagine. In reality, Pilate, I hold all the keys to this situation...' Scary stuff!

From that moment, Pilate really wanted Jesus set free. In fact, he probably wanted to do a runner! He just had no backbone. In the final analysis, he was not his own man. As soon as the mob shouted, 'You are no friend of Caesar!' Pilate caved in.

Popularity and survival before justice and truth!

I once knew two men who worked in a factory under a real bully. Both were believers. One, the older man, had been a believer for years and never said anything to his boss – preferring to slap him on the back and tell him how great he was.

The younger man had only just become a Christian. In the past he'd thought that the boss' bullying was a bit amusing – as long as he wasn't on the receiving end! But when he became a believer, he went straight up to his boss and told him what he thought, much to the older believer's shame. In fact, the younger guy just couldn't understand why his colleague had never said anything for all those years. He told him to his face that one of the reasons he had held back from making a decision to follow Jesus was the other guy's conduct towards the boss! How gutting would that feel... to hear that said to you?

As statesman Edmund Burke said, 'All that is necessary for the triumph of evil is that good men do nothing.'

The quiet life comes at what cost?

QUESTIONS

Before we start to get a bit tough on Pilate, we need to do a frank and honest assessment of our own lives. How many times have we not told the truth because, frankly, it's easier to be the nice guy?
Are you your own man, or a crowd follower?
How many times have we let something wrong continue in the workplace because we don't want a bad work review or face losing our job?

Don't be a Pilate! Get stuck in and do your bit.

LANCE

'FILTH HAD IMPRISONED ME...'

The naked women on the glossy pages were 'entirely beautiful and exciting'... but instinctively the seven-year-old Lance knew there was something forbidden about looking at them. He kept returning to the magazines over and over – but he kept them secret.

He was hooked. Porn became a serious addiction that was to dominate his adolescence, threaten his marriage and lead to years of counselling and therapy.

'From childhood on my view of women was skewed, fantasy-based and two-dimensional,' recalls Lance.

At boarding school it was 'normal' to share glossy girlie magazines – confirming Lance in patterns of regularly using porn.

'It became a standard component of my life – never challenged by parents or teachers.'

By the time Lance became a young professional in the stressful world of finance and IT, he was a regular subscriber to *Penthouse* magazine and sourcing more porn via videos. A colleague introduced him to the world of table dance bars – where he spent hundreds of dollars over the next few years. A lot of it was 'on expenses' as these 'gentlemen's clubs' were on the regular corporate entertainment circuit.

'I knew I'd crossed over into another whole area of sexual stimulation. When I wasn't at the office I was preoccupied with porn and finding the next conquest.'

Working in the US, he dated and married Gina – successfully keeping his secret other life from her.

'I planned to leave it all behind when I got married, but I found I couldn't, so I gave up on that idea. Instead, lies and deception remained an integral part of my relationship with Gina – covering up my behaviour and creating opportunities for nights on the town with the boys and my worsening hard core video addiction.'

But Gina began to suspect that something was wrong with their marriage. Lance just didn't seem interested in sex. Was something wrong with her?

'The truth was, my addiction to porn meant I was largely unsuccessful with the real intimacy of a close relationship with my wife. I was getting my sexual needs met by two-dimensional images.' The inevitable happened, five years into the marriage. Gina came across Lance's stash of videos and confronted him. She was devastated – as betrayed as if he had been having an affair.

'I was devastated, too. Deep down I had always really loved Gina – and now I knew my marriage was lost – and life with Gina and my two beautiful kids was history.'

Lance was totally unprepared for Gina's response. They spent the whole day struggling to talk about his problems – and then, her face streaming with tears, she instinctively got on her knees and prayed to God. It was a prayer of recommitment to the God she had known throughout her childhood but had wandered away from in her late teens.

'For the next couple of days Gina shared the good news about Jesus Christ with me. Every word from her lips was like honey. I heard how Jesus had died on the cross for me, how I could be forgiven and restored. Gina was prepared to forgive me. Forgive? How could she forgive me? I was expecting to be thrown out onto the street after years of violating all marital boundaries and living a life built on lies and deception. But through Gina I learned that God is the God of second chances, and that he could make me literally a new creature with a new nature. Astoundingly, my life's slate would be wiped completely and utterly clean. I could start over! What relief!'

Gina got out her Bible and Lance had the experience of the Scriptures coming to life as he heard them. He gave his

life to God – feeling as if he was standing under some kind of spiritual shower, being cleansed on the inside.

'I was literally washed of all the filth that had imprisoned me.'

It was a long road back. Lance soberly describes the struggle of letting go of the destructive behaviour patterns he'd indulged from his childhood. It took several years of counselling, with some lapses and plenty of tears along the way.

'Now I didn't want our marriage just to work – I wanted it to be the best it could be. But it wasn't easy. Gina's trust in me had been shattered and rebuilding it took time and commitment.'

These days Lance is understandably concerned for our sex-obsessed culture, particularly with the widespread use of that most dangerous porn provider, the Internet. So concerned, in fact, that early in 2007 he gave up his job to concentrate full time on setting up a charity that offers hope and restoration to people struggling with sex addictions.

'What people don't understand is that sex addiction is not primarily about sex; it's fundamentally an intimacy disorder. I guess we're all of us the walking wounded. We all have different levels of dysfunction and need God's grace. But the porn problem is really prevalent – sadly, even within the Church. Porn has become normalised. There are so few places to turn to for help in the UK and I hope to redress that imbalance.

'Truth is the foundational ingredient to all healthy relationships,' says Lance. And, taking his inspiration from Paul's teaching on how to win the battle against 'the spiritual forces of evil', he has named his charity Belt of Truth Ministries. **GB**

www.beltoftruth.org.uk

Who?	King of Kings, our master and commander, our captain
When?	He existed before creation and lives eternally
Why?	He's the source of all love, all goodness, all life
Where?	The whole Bible is his story, from Genesis to Revelation

JESUS

HE LAID DOWN HIS LIFE FOR YOU...

As King of Kings, he is mighty and powerful and will one day judge the nations.

Yet he is all-forgiving and all-gracious.

He burns with holiness – yet is filled with compassion.

He is the source of all our understanding of the qualities of nobility, heroism, sacrifice, honour, majesty, strength, integrity, mercy, authority, justice, righteousness and morality... and much more.

He is the source of life; Alpha and Omega, beginning and end.

He takes people's lives and turns them around.

He takes the sick and he heals them.

He takes the broken and he makes them whole.

He takes the self-sufficient and shows them their dependence on him.

He humbles the proud and shows mercy to the weak.

He uplifts the poor and challenges the rich.

He touches the untouchable and loves the unlovable.

He always had time for people: the outcast...
the prostitute... the small child... the lonely...
the sick...
He was there at the beginning and he will be there at
the end of time as we know it.
He will throw Satan and his demons into the lake of fire.
And all of us will one day kneel before him.
He laid down his life for you. Taking the pain and the
humiliation, he had you in his mind as he died. Yes, you!
He took the hit for all the stuff you have done that is an
offence to the God of the universe and he took the hit
for all the stuff that you are going to go on to do. **GB**

QUESTIONS

Is that the King you follow?

Is that the Jesus you serve?

Are you ready to go where he tells you to go and do what he asks you to do?

Do you live for him? And I mean, really live for him?

ACTIONS

Stop being lukewarm.

Stop making excuses for half-hearted discipleship.

Shake off your apathy.

Let go of your pride.

Yield everything to him:

• your wallet

• your pride

• your time

• your future

• your career

• your ego

Serve him, honour him and live your life to the full.

As believing men, we are a band of brothers. Let's be iron sharpening iron! Let's pursue the kingdom together!